More About Jesus Would I Know

by Johnie Edwards and John Isaac Edwards

ONE STONE
BIBLICAL RESOURCES

Published by:
One Stone Press
979 Lovers Lane
Bowling Green, KY 42103

Printed in the United States of America

ISBN 10: 1941422152
ISBN 13: 978-1-941422-15-1

Supplemental Materials Available:
PowerPoint slides for each lesson
Answer key
Downloadable PDF

ONE STONE
BIBLICAL RESOURCES

www.onestone.com

Table of Contents

Introduction

"And there are also many other things which Jesus did, the which, if they should be written every one, I suppose that even the world itself could not contain the books that should be written. Amen." — John 21:25

This Bible study takes a Biblical look at some things Jesus did and did not do, had and did not have, and will do.

Some Things Jesus Did (Part 1)

Prayed

1. "And when he had sent the multitudes away, he went up into a mountain apart to _____: and when evening was come he was there alone" (Matt. 14:23).

2. "Then cometh Jesus with them unto a place called Gethsemane, and saith unto the disciples, Sit ye here, while I go and _____ yonder" (Matt. 26:36).

3. Jesus not only prayed for himself; he also prayed for others: "I pray for them: I pray not for the world, but for _____ which thou hast given me; for they are thine" (Jn. 17:9).

4. Often our Lord would pick a _____ place to pray (Mk. 1:35).

5. Jesus left us an _____as he prayed (1 Pet. 2:21).

6. Not only did Jesus pray, He taught others how to _____ (Mt. 6:5-15).

7. We are also taught to pray: "_____ without ceasing" (1 Thess. 5:17). What did you learn from reading Philippians 4:6-7? _____

    _____

Practiced what He taught

1. Luke reported, as he wrote about Jesus: "The former treatise have I made, O Theophilus, of all that Jesus began both to _____ and _____" (Acts 1:1). Did you notice the order? Jesus first did and then he taught!

2. Now read Ezra 7:10 and Romans 2:21-22. Note the order: _____

    _____

Was obedient to His parents

1. We live in a society today where many children have no idea what parental obedience involves.

2. Jesus knew. Remember the time Jesus was left behind in Jerusalem (Lk. 2:42-43)? After finding Jesus, the Bible says: "And he went down with them, and came to Nazareth, and was _____" (Lk. 2:51).

3. This might be a good time to read, study and discuss what Paul said in Ephesians 6:1-4!

Grew

1. The Bible affirms in Luke 2:52 that Jesus "increased in..."

    _____ _____ _____ _____

2. Write a brief statement explaining what each of these mean.

    _____

    _____

    _____

    _____

3. The scripture places emphasis on our growth as well (1 Pet. 2:2). What does 2 Peter 3:18 tell Christians to grow in? _____

    _____

Paid taxes

1. The question was asked of Peter: "...Doth not your master pay tribute? What was Peter's answer? _____ How did Jesus get the money to pay this tribute? _____ (Mt. 17:24-27).

2. Find and note what W. E. Vine says about the word "tribute." _____

    _____

    _____

3. To see our obligations in this, please read Romans 13:1-7 and note what you learned from the reading: _____

_____

Wept

1. The Bible's shortest verse says: "Jesus wept." Take your concordance and find this reference. _____

2. What was the occasion where Jesus wept? _____

_____

3. Jesus showed compassion for others. Why does Matthew 9:36 say that Jesus was "moved with compassion?" _____

_____

4. The Lord's people must also be a people who show compassion for others. Paul wrote the Romans: "Rejoice with them that do _____, and _____ with them that _____" (Rom. 12:15).

5. Peter penned: "Finally, be ye all of one mind, _____ _____ one of another, love as brethren, be pitiful, be courteous" (1 Pet. 3:8).

6. What does 1 John 3:17-18 teach us about having compassion? _____

_____

Built His church

1. One of the greatest promises Jesus ever made was: "I will build _____ church...." (Mt. 16:18).

2. Read, study and discuss Matthew 16:13-20.

3. Please read these Bible passages, noting the relationship of Jesus to each:

Colossians 1:18 _____

Ephesians 5:23 _____

1 Corinthians 3:11 _____

4. From Romans 16:16, how is the church identified? _____

_____

5. From the prophecy of Isaiah 2:2-3 to Acts 2, show how all this came to be. _____

_____

_____

_____

_____

Some Things Jesus Did (Part 2)

Performed miracles

1. Being divine while on earth, Jesus was able to perform all kinds of miracles. John reported the "_____ of miracles did Jesus in Cana of Galilee...." (Jn. 2:11). Now read John 2:1-10 and discuss this miracle. _____

    _____

    _____

2. The reason for miracles was to cause men to "_____ on him!"

3. See if you can find and bring to class a list of different miracles performed by Jesus:

    _____

    _____

    _____

    _____

    _____

Overthrew the tables of money changers

1. Read Matthew 21:12-13 and be able to discuss in Bible class what is going on in this reference. _____

    _____

    _____

2. Where is Matthew 21:13 written in the Old Testament? _____

    _____

Taught and preached

1. Jesus was the master teacher of all time! The mountain message is one of His greatest (Mt. 5-7)!

2. Often it is said of Jesus: "...on the sabbath day he entered into the synagogue, and _____(Mk. 1:21).

3. Much of the teaching of our Lord was in parables. A parable is an earthly story designed to teach a spiritual truth. "And he taught them many things by _____" (Mk. 4:2). Find a parable of Jesus and be able to tell the class where it is found and what lesson is learned from it. _____

    _____

    _____

    _____

4. Jesus used questions in his teaching. A good example: When the chief priests, the scribes and the elders asked Jesus, "By what authority doest thou these things? And who gave thee this authority to do these things?" Jesus answered, "I will also _____ _____, and answer me, and I will tell you by what authority I do these things" (Mk. 11:27-33).

5. We would do well to learn how to ask good questions in our teaching.

Washed disciples' feet

1. Jesus was humble and taught His disciples to be humble.

2. During one of the Passover feasts, Jesus "began to wash the disciples' _____, and to wipe them with the towel wherewith he was girded" (Jn. 13:1-17).

3. Foot washing is not connected with worship; it was an act of hospitality connected with "_____" (1 Tim. 5:10).

4. The washing of feet was done in Old Testament times. See if you can find a reference of that: _____

Was baptized

1. You can read the account of Jesus being baptized in Matthew 3:13-17.

2. Who baptized Jesus? _____

3. Since Jesus had no sins, why was He baptized? _____

_____

What does this mean? _____

_____

4. Prove that Jesus was immersed when He was baptized. _____

_____

Did His Father's will

1. Jesus was obedient to the will of His Father. The Hebrew writer recorded: "Then said

he, Lo, I come to _____ ,

O God...." (Heb. 10:9).

2. Jesus could be heard saying: "...not as I _____, but as thou wilt" (Mt. 26:39).

3. Just as Jesus did the will of the Father, we must also learn to do the same. "Not every

one that saith unto me, Lord, Lord, shall enter into the kingdom of heaven; but he

that _____ of my Father which is in heaven" (Mt. 7:21).

Overcame Satan's temptations

1. First, read Matthew 4:1-11 and Luke 4:1-13.

2. Please answer these questions:

Why was this a good time to tempt Jesus? _____

How many ways was Jesus tempted? _____

Could Jesus have given in to these temptations? _____

What had Jesus hid in His heart to help him say no to these temptations?
(Ps. 119:11) _____

What does the phrase "it is written" mean? _____

Ever wonder why Satan didn't try one more time to tempt Jesus (1 Jn. 2:15-17)?

_____

From Luke's account, might the devil return to tempt Jesus again?_____

3. Discuss: How can we overcome the temptations of the devil today? Read James 1:12-15, James 4:7-8; 1 Corinthians 10:13. _____

_____

Took note of little children

1. Little children were special to Jesus. He often took notice of them.

2. "Then were there brought unto him little children, that he should put his hands on them, and pray: and the disciples rebuked them. But Jesus said, Suffer _____

_____ and forbid them not, to come unto me: for of such is the kingdom

of heaven. And he _____ his _____ on them and departed" (Mt. 19:13-15).

3. What did Jesus do when the apostles were saying, "Who is the greatest in the kingdom of heaven (Mt. 18:1-6)? _____

_____

4. What does Psalm 127:3 say about children? _____

_____

5. Our children are the future generation. Just as Joel 1:3 says, "Tell your _____ of it, and let your children _____ their children, and _____ children another generation."

Some Things Jesus Did (Part 3)

Calmed the winds and the sea

1. Since "the sea is his, and he made it: and his hands formed the dry land" (Ps. 95:5), He can calm such. One time Jesus "arose, and _____ the winds and the sea; and there was _____ " (Mk. 8:23-27).

2. Jesus being able to calm the winds and the sea, as they were obedient unto him, caused men to marvel, saying, "What manner of man is this, that even the winds and the sea _____ him" (Mk. 8:27)! Surely, He was divine while on earth!

Spoke with authority

1. Jesus claimed to have "all power (authority)...in heaven and in earth" (Mt. 28:18).

2. When Jesus taught, how did He teach (Mt. 7:29)? _____
    _____

3. "The officers answered, _____ man spake like this man" (Jn. 7:46).

4. There are expressions of the authority of Jesus on the pages of inspiration. Read and list the phrase indicating authority.

    John 2:5 _____

    Luke 5:5 _____

5. One of the great problems facing the Lord's people is that of respect for divine authority today!

Taught in parables

1. A parable is an earthly story designed to teach a spiritual truth. Much of the teaching of Jesus was in parables.

2. Matthew 13:3 says: "And he spake _____
    unto them in parables...."

3. A good example of his parable teaching is the parable of the sower (Lk. 8:5-15). Read
    and discuss this in Bible class.

4. Bring to class your favorite parable and tell the class where it is located in the Bible
    and what it teaches. _____
    _____

5. See if you can find the number of New Testament parables. _____

6. Are there any parables we cannot use today? _____
    If so, which ones? _____

7. Why did Jesus teach in parables? Find the reference to this question and discuss in
    class: _____

Instituted the Lord's Supper

1. The accounts of Jesus instituting the Lord's Supper are found in Matthew 26:17-
    29; Mark 14:22-25 and Luke 22:7-20. Read each of these carefully and answer and
    discuss these questions:

    What was being eaten? _____

    How many elements in the Lord's Supper? _____

    Name them: _____

    What is the "cup"? _____

    What does each of the elements remind us of? _____
    _____

    What does 1 Corinthians 11: 20-34 teach us? _____
    _____

    Does 1 Corinthians 11 tell us when the Lord's Supper is to be eaten?_____

Where do we learn when the communion is to be partaken? _____

When is that? _____

2. We must ever be diligent to keep the Lord's Supper on the Lord's Day as prescribed by our Lord!

Fulfilled the law of Moses

1. Jesus affirmed: "Think not that I am come to destroy the law, or the prophets: I am not come to destroy, _____ For verily I say unto you, Till heaven and earth pass, one jot or one tittle shall in no wise pass from the law till all be fulfilled" (Mt. 5:17-18).

2. What does the word "fulfill" mean? _____

3. Define a "jot" _____

4. What is a "tittle?" _____

5. Read and discuss these passages of scripture:

John 1:17 _____

_____

Romans 7:1-7 _____

_____

2 Corinthians 3:3-16 _____

_____

Galatians 3:19-25 _____

_____

Galatians 4:21-31 _____

_____

Ephesians 2:15 _____

_____

Galatians 6:2 _____

_____

Colossians 2:14-17 _____

_____

Hebrews 8:4-13 _____

_____

Hebrews 10:1-4 _____

_____

Hebrews 10:9-10 _____

_____

6. Write a summary of what all the above scriptures teach. _____

_____

_____

Some Things Jesus Did (Part 4)

Made provisions for His mother

1. At His crucifixion: "Now there stood by the cross of Jesus his mother, and his mother's sister, Mary the wife of Cleophas, and Mary Magdalene. When Jesus therefore saw his mother, and the disciple standing by, whom he loved, he saith unto his mother, Woman, behold thy son! Then saith he to the disciple, Behold _____! And from that hour that disciple took her unto his own home" (Jn. 19:25-27). Jesus was concerned about His mother's welfare after he was gone.

2. Children need to have care and concern for their parents as well. Paul told Timothy to teach, "But if any widow have children or nephews, let them learn first to shew piety at home, and to requite _____ · for that is good and acceptable before God" (1 Tim. 5:4).

3. Our mothers and fathers took care of us when we could not care for ourselves; now, it may be our turn to care for them!

Attended a wedding

1. The Hebrew writer penned: "Marriage is _____ in all, and the bed undefiled: but whoremongers and adulterers God will judge" (Heb. 13:4).

2. Jesus attended a wedding in Cana of Galilee. "And the third day there was a _____ in Cana of Galilee; and the mother of Jesus was there" (Jn. 2:1). He must have approved of marriage!

3. We are living in a society where people are just living together, unmarried. This arrangement may be approved by many, but it is still sinful! Paul taught the Corinthians, "Nevertheless, to avoid fornication, let _____ _____ have _____ _____ wife, and let _____ _____ have her _____ husband" (1 Cor. 7:2).

By the way, this is still so!

4. Our young people need to be taught, "that he which made them at the beginning made them male and female, And said, For this cause shall a man leave father and mother, and shall cleave to his wife: and they twain shall be one flesh? Wherefore they are no more twain, but one flesh. What therefore God hath joined together _____ _____ _____ put _____" (Mt. 19:4-6).

5. Marriage is "until death do we part!" Jesus taught, "And I say unto you, Whosoever shall put away his wife, except it be _____ _____, and shall marry another, committeth adultery: and who marrieth her which is put away doth commit adultery" (Mt. 19:9).

Amazed and astonished people

1. The things that Jesus did stood out from that of others, and people wondered.

2. When Jesus taught, it was said, "When his disciples heard it, they were _____ amazed" (Mt. 19:25).

3. Jesus "rebuked the unclean spirit, and healed the child, and delivered him again to his father. And they were _____ at the mighty power of God. But while they wondered every one at all things which _____ _____" (Lk. 9:42-43).

4. The scriptures tell us, "It came to pass, when Jesus had ended these sayings, the people were _____ at his _____: For he taught them as one having _____, and not as the scribes" (Mt. 7:24-29)!

Commissioned the apostles

1. Before Jesus ascended back to His Father, he gave the apostles a world-wide commission.

2. Read, study and discuss in Bible class the three accounts of this charge:

    Matthew 28:18-20 _____

    _____

Mark 16:15-16 _____

_____

Luke 24:46-49_____

_____

3.   Now, from Acts 1:7-8 and Acts 2-19, by calling attention to cases of New Testament conversion, learn how this great commission was carried out as the word was heard, believed and obeyed, adding the saved to the church!

Finished His earthly work

1.   One of the utterances of Jesus on the cross was, "It is _____: and he bowed his head, and gave up the ghost" (Jn. 19:30).

2.   "These words spake Jesus, and lifted up his eyes to heaven, and said...I have glorified thee on the earth: I _____ _____ the work which thou gavest me to do" (Jn. 17:1-4).

3.   Those who teach that Jesus has unfinished work to do on earth and will come back to this earth to do other works need to take a look at and explain what Jesus meant when He said He "finished the work thou gavest me to do!"

Died, was buried, was resurrected, ascended

1.   The gospel of Christ is about the finality of the things Jesus did.

2.   A reading of 1 Corinthians 15:1-7, Acts 1:9-11, John 19 and Luke 24:1-12 will give us a vivid picture of the death, burial, resurrection and ascension of Jesus.

3.   This gospel is God's power "to save" (Rom. 1:16), and may we get to preaching it far and near!

Some Things Jesus Did Not Do (Part 1)

Give up His deity

1. We have been told that when Jesus came to earth, He gave up His deity and became as an ordinary man like you and me. The Bible teaches that Jesus was both "the Son of _____" (Mk. 14:41) and "the Son of _____" (Mk. 1:1).

2. While on earth, Jesus was 100% man and 100% God!

3. Those who teach that Jesus gave up His deity when He came to earth misuse Philippians 2:5-8. A reading of the passage says nothing about Jesus giving up His deity. He left heaven and came to earth, thus giving up what He had in heaven.

Commit sin

1. The Hebrew writer said that Jesus "was in all points tempted like as we are, yet _____ sin" (Heb. 4:15).

2. Peter penned, "Who did _____ _____, neither was guile found in his mouth" (1 Pet. 2:22).

3. Paul said it this way: "For he made him to be sin for us, who _____ no _____; that we might be made the righteousness of God in him" (2 Cor. 5:21).

4. When His enemies "sought false witness against Jesus, to put him to death; But found _____: yea, though many false witnesses came, yet found they none. At the last came two false witnesses" (Mt. 26:59-60).

5. When Jesus was accused before Pilate, "Then said Pilate to the chief priests and to the people, _____ in this man" (Lk. 23:1-4; Jn. 19:4).

6. We, being human, are guilty of sin. "For all have _____, and come short of the glory of God" (Rom. 3:23). John wrote, "If we say that we have no sin, we _____ ourselves, and the truth is not in us" (1 Jn. 1:8).

7. This is one reason Jesus "came to seek and to save the lost" (Lk. 19:10).

Make Himself of reputation

1. Paul taught concerning Christ, "Who being in the form of God, thought it not robbery to be equal with God: But made of himself of _____ reputation, and took upon him the form of a servant" (Phil. 2:7).

2. Mark recorded, "For even the Son of man came not to be ministered unto, but to minister, and to give his life a ransom for many" (Mk. 10:45).

3. Jesus never came to earth to be popular! He never sought such.

Retaliate

1. Some, when mistreated, want to get even. Jesus did not do that. 1 Peter 2:23 says, "Who, when he was reviled, reviled not again: when he suffered, he _____ not; but committed himself to him that judgeth righteously."

2. We all need to learn: "Dearly beloved, _____ not yourselves, but rather give place unto wrath: for it is written, Vengeance is _____; I will repay, saith the Lord" (Rom. 12:19).

3. It is not ours, vengeance belongs to the Lord, and He will take care of that!

4. Instead of retaliating when done wrong, what did Paul tell the Roman Christians to do in Romans 12:20-21? _____

_____

Tolerate error or overlook sin

1. He said unto them that sold doves in the temple, "Take these things _____; make not my Father's house an house of merchandise" (Jn. 2:16).

2. Jesus admonished the woman taken in adultery: "go, and sin no more" (Jn. 8:11).

3   We must not allow error to go on unnoticed. Paul told the Galatian Christians, "To whom we gave place by subjection, no, not for an _____..." (Gal. 2:5).

Build more than one church

1. Some want to credit the Lord with having established all the different churches that exist today. He only built one church: His! The Lord said, "I will build _____ church" (Mt. 16:18). Paul pointed out, "There is _____ (Ep. 4:4) "which is the _____" (Col. 1:24).

2. When this is added up, how many churches do you get out of this? _____! Are you a member of this church? _____

Some Things Jesus Did Not Do (Part 2)

Please Himself

1. Jesus did not come to do His own will. His petition was, "not my will, but thine be done" (Lk. 22:42). "Then said he, Lo, I come to do thy will, O God" (Heb. 10:9). Romans 15:3 teaches, "For even Christ _____ _____ _____..." The Lord said, "for I do always those _____ that please him" (Jn. 8:29).

2. We live in a self-centered world today and often think only of self.

3. By the way, who are you trying to please? _____

Teach one thing and practice another

1. Some try to teach without doing. This will not work! The life of Jesus was consistent with His teaching. "Jesus began both to _____ and _____" (Acts 1:1).

2. For example, Jesus loved (Jn. 15:13) and taught _____ (Jn.13:34-35). He forgave (Lk. 23:34) and taught _____ (Mt. 6:14-15). And on that goes!

3. We need to learn to "go and do likewise" (Rom. 2:21-22).

Apologize for His teaching

1. Some today think they have to apologize when folks become upset with the truth. The Lord didn't. As He was teaching, His disciples came and said, "Knowedst thou that the Pharisees were _____, after they heard this saying? But he answered and said, Every plant, which my heavenly Father hath not planted, _____ be _____ up. Let them alone: they be blind leaders of the blind. And if the blind lead the blind, _____ shall fall into the ditch" (Mt. 12:12-14).

2. There is entirely too much tread-lightly, speak-softly kind of preaching going on today!

Come down from the cross

1. There were those who taunted Him saying, "Thou that destroyest the temple, and buildest it in three days, _____ _____. If thou be the Son of God, _____ down from the cross" (Mt. 27:40). He could have come down. Jesus said: "Thinkest thou that I cannot now pray to my Father, and he shall presently give me more that than _____" (Mt. 26:53)?

2. The Holy Spirit revealed, "he by the grace of God should taste _____ for every man" (Heb. 2:9).

Stay in the grave

1. The musical *Jesus Christ Superstar* left Jesus dead in the grave! The angel said, "He is not here: he is _____, as he said" (Mt. 28:6). Peter preached, "his soul was not left in hell (*hades*), neither did his flesh see corruption" (Acts 2:27).

2. The resurrection is proof that Jesus was who he said he was. "And declared to be the Son of God, with power, according to the spirit of holiness, by the _____ from the dead" (Rom. 1:3).

3. The resurrection of Jesus also assures our resurrection!

Personally baptize

1. Jesus taught, "He that believeth and is baptized shall be saved" (Mk. 16:16).

2. Jesus did not personally baptize. It is written, "When therefore the Lord knew how the Pharisees had heard that Jesus made and baptized more disciples than John, Though Jesus _____ baptized not, but his disciples" (Jn. 4:1-2). Jesus preached and taught many; others seemed to have done the immersion of His converts.

Return silently or invisibly

1. One of the great promises of the New Testament is when Jesus said, "I will _____ again" (Jn. 14:3). Some have tried to convince us that Jesus has already returned—only a few to none saw or heard Him. The scriptures will not allow such a conclusion!

2. The Bible connects "His coming" with "the _____" (1 Cor. 15:23-24).

3. The second coming of Christ will be audible, "for the trumpet shall _____" (1 Cor. 15:52).

4. His coming will be visible; "_____ eye shall see him" (Rev. 1:7).

5. The second coming of Jesus is yet to be, and all of us need to "be ready" for it (Mt. 24:44)!

6. By the way, are you ready? If not, you need to obey the gospel of Christ now, as the Corinthians did: "hearing, believed and were baptized" (Acts 18:8)!

Some Things Jesus Had

A virgin birth

1. Hundreds of years before the birth of Jesus, Isaiah, prophesied, "Therefore the Lord himself shall give you a sign: Behold a _____ shall conceive, and bear a son, and shall call his name Immanuel" (Isa. 7:14).

2. The birth of Jesus was a normal birth. The miracle concerning His birth was the conception: "for that which is conceived in her is of the _____ _____ (Mt. 1:20).

3. Matthew sanctioned this birth as he said, "And she shall bring forth a son, and thou shalt call his name Jesus: For he shall save his people from their sins. Now all this was done, that it might be _____ which was spoke of the Lord by the _____, saying..." (Mt. 1:21-22). Then Matthew quotes _____ (Mt. 1:23)!

4. Some Bible translations say "young woman" instead of "virgin." What is wrong with this? _____
   _____

5. Many today reject the virgin birth of Jesus and teach men so!

Care and compassion

1. Jesus had compassion and care for others. When Jesus saw "sheep having no _____" the Bible says, "He was _____ with compassion" (Mt. 9:36).

2. Jesus cared. We need to sing often: "Does Jesus Care?"

3. Paul wrote the Corinthians, "That there should be no schism in the body; but that _____ should have the same _____ one for another" (1 Cor. 12:25).

4. In fact, if "one member suffer, _____ the members suffer with it; or one member be honoured, all the _____ rejoice with it" (1 Cor. 12:26).

A short earthly life

1. Jesus lived on this earth for about 33 years. Yet He accomplished a lot in this short period of time. What does John 21:25 say about what He did? _____

    _____

2. It's not how long a person lives but how well!

Lots of followers

1. When He would go into a place, crowds pressed upon Him. "And when they could not come nigh unto him for the _____, they uncovered the roof where he was" (Mk. 2:4).

2. Matthew 8:1 records, "When he was come down from the mountain, _____ _____ followed him" (Mt. 8:1).

3. It seems to be getting more difficult to get folks to follow the Lord and His teachings. Do you see this? _____

Knowledge of man

1. Don't forget that Jesus was at the creation of man (Gen. 1:26-27; Col. 1:16)!

2   John reported, "And needeth not that any should testify of man: for he _____ what was in man" (Jn. 2:25).

3. Jesus knew what men were thinking without their speaking. Jesus could "perceive" and ask, "...why reason ye among yourselves..." (Mt. 16:8). Matthew recorded, "And Jesus knowing their _____ said, Wherefore think ye evil in your hearts" (Mt. 9:4).

4. So, never think that the Lord doesn't know what you are doing and thinking!

A heavenly Father

1. In teaching men how to pray, Jesus addressed the prayer to "Our Father which art in heaven" (Mt. 6:9).

2. "Every plant which my heavenly Father hath not planted, shall be rooted up" (Mt. 15:13).

3. If you are in God's family, you can call God your heavenly Father, too!

Pre-earth existence

1. Jesus has always been; He is eternal. John said of Jesus, "In the beginning was the Word, and the Word was _____ God, and the Word was God. The same was in the beginning _____ God" (Jn. 1:1-2).

2. Paul indicated the pre-earth existence of Jesus when he penned Philippians 2:5-8. Read it!

3. Just as John said, "And the Word was made _____, and dwelt among us, (and we beheld his glory, the glory as of the only begotten of the Father,) full of grace and truth" (Jn. 1:14).

4. This teaching knocks the props from underneath the false concept that Jesus was a "created being!"

Power to forgive sins

1. It is written in Matthew 9:6, "But that ye may know that the Son of man _____ _____ on earth to forgive sins, (then saith he to the sick of the palsy,) Arise, take up thy bed, and go unto thine house" (Jn. 9:6).

2. Do you know any mere man, like you and me, that can do this?

A short ministry

1. How old was Jesus when He began His ministry? _____

2. This left only about _____ years for Him to do His work on earth (Lk. 3:23).

3. How did John describe what he did in these few years (Jn. 21:25)? _____

_____

_____

Thorns for a crown

1. John said, "And the soldiers platted a _____ of _____, and put it on his head, and they put on him a purple robe" (Jn. 19:2).

2. Add to this, "Then Pilate therefore took Jesus, and _____ Him" (Jn. 19:1). What does John 18:22 say they did to Jesus? _____

_____

3. Jesus wore a crown of thorns that we might have the right to wear the "crown of life" (Rev. 2:10)!

Some Things Jesus Did Not Have

An earthly father

1. Even though Joseph is said, in a sense, to be the father of Jesus (Lk. 2:41, 48), God is His real Father. Jesus often referred to God as His _____ (Lk. 23:46).

2. Every child today needs a father figure in the home.

Desire to get even

1. We are living in a "get even" society. Jesus had no such disposition. In fact, the Bible cites, "Who, when he was reviled, reviled not _____; when he suffered, he threatened _____; but committed himself to him that judgeth righteously" (1 Pet. 2:23).

2. Parents would do well to teach their children this attitude.

A place to lay His head

1. The Holy Spirit reported, "And Jesus said unto him, The foxes have _____, and the birds of the air have _____; but the Son of man hath not where to _____ his head" (Mt. 8:20).

2. The Bible teaches, "For ye know the grace of our Lord Jesus Christ, that, though he was _____, yet for your sakes he became _____, that ye through his poverty might be rich" (2 Cor. 8:9).

3. While sleeping in your Sleep Number® bed, do you ever take the time to think about what Jesus did for you?

Respect of persons

1. The Lord is an impartial Lord. Paul wrote the Romans, "For there is _____ respect of persons with God" (Rom. 2:11).

2. Read Acts 10:34-35, noting how Peter began his sermon at the house of Cornelius.

_____

_____

3. Read James 2:1-9 and be ready to discuss in class.

Knowledge of the time of the second coming

1. Mark said that Jesus did not know "that day and hour" (Mk. 13:32) when the second coming will be.

2. It is possible that Jesus may have chosen not to know this time. What do you think?

_____

_____

Long earthly life

1. Today, most people live more than twice the years that Jesus lived.

2. He lived for about 33 years on this earth.

3. Yet He accomplished more than anyone who ever lived on this earth (Jn. 21:25)!

4. Ever think about how big the book would be if all Jesus did had been written down?

5. Some die young, some old. It's not a matter of living-years, it's a matter of how well we redeem the time. In reality, life is short, death is sure and eternity is long. So we all need to be ready, all the time!

Some Things Jesus Will Do

Come again

1. As Jesus informed His disciples of His departure to the Father, He promised: "I will come again" (Jn. 14:3).

2. Angels said at His ascension, He "shall so _____ in like manner as ye have seen him go into heaven" (Acts 1:11).

3. Do we know when he will return? _____ Read Mark 13:32 to learn the answer.

4. How does 2 Peter 3:10 describe His second coming? _____

   _____

5. What does this do to so-called time setters? _____

   _____

Bring those who sleep in Him

1. Paul comforted the Thessalonians concerning their fellow Christians who had passed from this life. He said, "that ye sorrow not, even as others which have no hope. For if we believe that Jesus died and rose again, even so them also which _____ in Jesus will God bring with him" (1 Thess. 4:14).

2. What does "the dead in Christ shall rise first" mean (1 Thess. 4:16)? _____

   _____

Raise the dead

1. Jesus said, "Marvel not at this: for the hour is coming, in the which _____ that are in the graves shall hear his voice. And shall come forth, they that have done good, unto the resurrection of _____; and they that have done evil, unto the resurrection of _____" (Jn. 5:28-29).

2. Did you notice that "all" dead will be raised at the same hour?

3. According to Acts 24:15, there will be _____ resurrection. This means there will only be one general resurrection!

Judge all

1. Jesus "was ordained of God to be the judge of the quick and the dead" (Acts 10:42).

2. "For we must _____ appear before the judgment seat of Christ; that _____ _____ may receive the things done in his body, according to that he hath done, whether it be good or bad" (2 Cor. 5:10).

3. Matthew 25:31-46 gives us a snapshot of the final judgment. Read and discuss this in class.

Reward every man

1. Rewards will be handed out at the judgment. Matthew 16:27 records, "For the Son of man shall come in the glory of his Father with his angels, and _____ he shall reward _____ man according to his works."

2. This shows that there will be no two-stage coming of our Lord, as we are often taught!

Put down His rule

1. Jesus is reigning now; that reign is temporary. It is written: "...when he shall have put down all rule and authority and power. For he must reign _____ he hath put all enemies under his feet" (1 Cor. 15:24-25).

2. This will take place when "he hath put all enemies under his feet. The last enemy that shall be destroyed is _____ (1 Cor. 15:25-26). This means as long as there are those who are dead, Christ will reign. But when He comes, there will be no dead; they will have been resurrected!

Deliver up the kingdom

1. Paul penned, "Then cometh the end, when he shall have _____ up the kingdom to God, even the Father" (1 Cor. 15:24-25).

2. We are often told that, at His coming, Jesus will set up an earthly kingdom. Not so! It has already been set up. If you know the difference between "deliver up" and "set up," you will never fall for the false doctrine of premillennalism!

3. Thus, it is vital that we be in the kingdom, which is the New Testament Church, by being "born again" (Jn. 3:3-5)!

Conclusion

1. Having learned some things Jesus will do at His second coming, it behooves each of us to obey His words (Jn. 12:48) and be ready for His coming.

2. Thanks for taking your time for this Bible study.

www.ingramcontent.com/pod-product-compliance
Lightning Source LLC
Chambersburg PA
CBHW081228040426
42445CB00016B/1918